Just Like Me

Stories and Self-Portraits
by Fourteen Artists

Edited by Harriet Rohmer

Children's Book Press
San Francisco, California

Tomie Arai

New York is a wonderful place to live because there is so much to look at. When I was a little girl, I would spend hours looking out the window of our apartment. I always thought that windows were a place to dream.

As I got older, I could walk for hours around the different neighborhoods of the city, and I started sketching the people I saw. I wanted to be like the painters Diego Rivera and Romare Bearden and the Japanese printmaker, Hokusai, who really looked at the world around them and tried to record the way that people lived.

This is a picture of me looking out the window. Or maybe it is a picture that lets you look into a window at me. I am dreaming that I am a little girl again, surrounded by memories that float across the page like the people who pass me on the crowded streets of the city.

Tomie Arai is a painter, printmaker, and mixed-media artist. She is a recent recipient of a National Endowment for the Arts Visual Arts Fellowship, and her work is in the collection of New York's Museum of Modern Art. Tomie has two children and lives in New York City where she was born in 1949.

Enrique Magoya

Enrique Chagoya

Sometimes I get an idea and laugh about it, and that gives me the green light to go ahead and paint it. But not always. There's no formula for making art. Art for me is an act of freedom, an act of intuition, an act of trust in myself. Art is also a way for me to express my concerns, dreams, and hopes for the society in which we live.

I try to have some sense of humor in my art and in my life. Art and humor can be our best friends when we go through difficult times, and it is even better if you add your favorite music to dance. For me it is salsa music. I enjoy dancing with the great sound of percussion and some loud trumpets. Here I am dancing with my wife, Kara, who is also an artist. I dressed her like a butterfly and made me look all raggedy—because the picture is more fun that way!

Enrique Chagoya teaches painting, drawing, and printmaking at Stanford University. His paintings and graphics are shown in museums and galleries throughout the world. He was born in Mexico City in 1953, moved to the San Francisco Bay Area in 1979, and now lives in San Francisco, California.

Carmen Lomas Garza

Most of my paintings are from my recollections of my childhood in south Texas where I was born and raised. My memories of celebrations are very vivid because I usually had a new special outfit sewed by my mother. My favorite was the turquoise cotton organza dress she made for my graduation from elementary school. Every year she sewed new school clothes for all five of us kids, but the funniest were the flannel pajamas in our choice of colors and patterns.

When I was a young girl, I taught myself how to draw clothes for my paper dolls so they could have any dress I wanted—a flamenco dancer's dress or a dress from Mexico called a China Poblana with lots of shiny sequins. To this day, my favorite thing to paint is clothing.

My mother was the first person I saw paint. She was the one who inspired me to become an artist.

Carmen Lomas Garza is one of the first Mexican American artists to receive national recognition. Her paintings have been shown in galleries and museums throughout the United States. She was born in Kingsville, Texas, in 1948 and now lives in San Francisco, California.

Maya Christina Gonzalez

One night when I was five years old, I woke up and saw a light shining brightly in the corner of my room. Some people said it was an angel. Some people said it was a ghost. All I know is it made me feel really happy, like I was special. After I saw that light, everything I looked at was brighter. I wanted to make art so I could show people what I was seeing and feeling.

In my painting I show the light shining from my heart. The words around the border are things that I love, like polka dots and fire, and ways that I feel, like loud and hungry. I stuck paintbrushes and pencils in my hair because I wanted to look good for my picture. The whole picture is lopsided because that's how it came out of the Xerox machine and I like it that way! Some of my best paintings happen by accident. You just never know.

Maya Christina Gonzalez is a painter who loves to share her art with children. Her work is shown in several West Coast galleries. She was born in Lancaster, California, in 1964 and now lives in San Francisco, California.

nancy Hom

I was born in a poor village in China where everyone worked hard in the fields. I came to America at the age of five. My brothers and I did not have many toys, and our parents were too busy to pay much attention to us. I had to invent a world of my own through pictures. I used the brightest crayons I could find to create scenes from my imagination.

I like to draw flat shapes that fit together like jigsaw puzzles. My artwork is very simple and graceful, with curves like the edges of clouds. I am like that—soft, gentle, quiet, but strong at the same time. I express my strength through bold colors and patterns that jump out and grab your attention. This portrait has leaves of bamboo in it because bamboo also comes from China. It is strong but it can bend when it needs to, just like me.

Nancy Hom is an artist, mother, designer, and the Executive Director of Kearny Street Workshop, an Asian American arts organization. She was born in Toisan, China, in 1949, grew up in New York City, and now lives in San Francisco, California.

George Littlechild

When I was a boy, people knew I was Indian (or First Nations, as we say in Canada) because I had the features of my Indian mother. As I got older, people weren't sure anymore. "You sure are exotic looking," they told me. "Are you Spanish? Italian? Portuguese?" I was looking more like my white father. But since both my parents were dead and I was living with my Dutch foster family, I was very confused about who I was. No one ever told me then that I was mixed-blood.

Sometimes I look Indian now, but sometimes I don't. My looks change according to my mood. That's why I've made these four different self-portraits. It took me many years to accept my features. Then one day I decided that I had to love myself just the way I am. I'm a rainbow man, with a half of this and a quarter of that, and a dash of a mixture of everything!

George Littlechild is a painter, printmaker, and mixed-media artist whose works are exhibited in galleries and museums throughout the world. A member of the Plains Cree Nation of Canada, he was born in Edmonton, Alberta, in 1958 and now lives in Vancouver, British Columbia.

NORMAL PUBLIC LIBRARY
NORMAL, ILLINOIS

Stephen Von Mason

I always loved making art. My earliest drawings were of rodeo horses and cowboys—mainly because of a book I had read about rodeo riders. The book had many wonderful drawings, and I would copy them over and over.

In junior high I loved to draw football players, and my school would hang my pictures in the display cases. Those were real fun times for me because my friends and I were always busy making things. We made bows and arrows and crossbows. We carved heads and flutes out of wood. I painted model cars, and everyone wanted me to draw their portrait.

When I went to college I decided to be a painter and printmaker, and that's when I found out that making art was more than just reproducing what I saw in front of me. I started making abstract art and art from my imagination. I learned to be true to my vision, and I let the world know how I see things!

Stephen Von Mason is a painter, printmaker, and fine-art framer whose work is shown in many galleries. He was born in South Bend, Indiana, in 1954 and now lives in Oakland, California.

Rodolfo Morales

All my life I have painted scenes from my little Mexican town of Ocotlán. When I was a boy, Ocotlán was still feeling the effects of the Mexican Revolution. We were very isolated. The train that stopped in our town twice each day was our only connection with modern life.

I remember that once an airplane passed overhead, surprizing the entire town. It was an American who had flown off course and made a forced landing behind the graveyard. He didn't speak Spanish, and only one person spoke English. He caused such a commotion that when he tried to take off, someone threw himself on the plane, not wanting it to leave, and there was almost a huge accident. You see, there weren't any movies, we didn't get any newspapers, and very few people knew that airplanes existed.

That's me on the left looking up at the pilot.

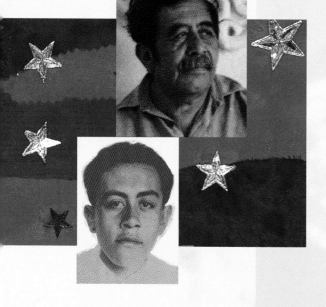

Rodolfo Morales is one of the most important artists in modern Mexico. His paintings and collages are shown internationally. He was born in Ocotlán, Mexico, in 1925, lived in Mexico City for many years, and now lives in Ocotlán. (He never had his picture taken as a child. His first photo, shown here, was taken when he was eighteen.)

Mira Reisberg

Welcome to my world! The dolphins are from my childhood in Australia where they saved children from shark attacks. These fun-loving dolphins are chasing after a juicy tuna lunch!

My paintings have beauty and magic for me. The desert blooms with barely any water. The cacti have prickles to protect themselves. My Jewish face has laughter and sadness. Guido and Possum, my funny, mischievous cats, love sneaking into my paintings. My boyfriend, Guy, and I are laughing from a flying heart floating across a fake leopard-print shirt.

There's a family portrait on the table. My mother and father were Holocaust survivors who came to Australia after the war. When my mom gave me my first art supplies, she said, "I can't give you a beautiful world, but you can make one for yourself." Being an artist has brought me much happiness, which I try to share. I can't imagine anything more wonderful—other than maybe being a dolphin.

Mira Reisberg is an artist, designer, and art teacher who loves to create art projects with children. She was born in Melbourne, Australia, in 1955 and now lives in San Francisco, California.

JoeSam.

POW!! When I was eight, I was considered a little rowdy, and I used to think I was cool. One day, I was hanging with my friend, Seawolf, and was late for school. A girl named Margaret finked to the teacher and I threatened to beat her up. After school, everyone was on the playground to watch the fight. Before I could even make a fist, Margaret whacked me in the eye with her book bag! I saw lots of stars and colors, and to this day all my paintings have lots of color in them. It's OK—I love to use lots of colors in my work; it makes me and other people laugh and smile. Colors are used by Third World cultures, and my art always reflects that.

And about Margaret—the next day we apologized to each other. After that we became best friends.

JoeSam. is a mixed-media artist with a strong love of Third World cultures. Known for his innovative public art sculptures, JoeSam. is also an internationally recognized painter. He was born in Harlem, New York, in 1939 and now lives in San Francisco, California.

Elly Simmons

When I was little, my mother strolled me around museums to see art. The walls of our home were covered with her paintings, with colorful posters of Mexican art, and with prints by Ben Shahn showing people at work. These images stayed with me, shaping who I am.

I paint my love of life! I paint pomegranates, birds, mountains, and people. I paint what gives me joy, or makes me sad or angry. I paint to protest homelessness, war, and injustice, and to celebrate the beauty of a sunflower outside my door.

When my daughter was born, brilliant suns burst into my paintings. Now I gather bright fabrics and photos to piece together a quilt of my Jewish family history. In this painting, my grandmother (as a baby) and my great-grandparents in the pomegranates honor my roots. My parents, in the yellow sun, are my source of life. They gave me love and the encouragement to celebrate life through art!

Elly Simmons is an artist and a community activist. Her paintings, prints, and tapestries are shown internationally. She was born in New York City in 1955, grew up in San Francisco, and now lives in Lagunitas, California.

Daryl Wells

When I was growing up, I didn't understand why the crayon labeled "flesh" in my crayon box wasn't the color of my skin. As a way of proving that my color was also beautiful and real, I went through all my favorite storybooks and colored in the characters with the brown crayon. In this way I was able to relate to them as if they really were part of my world.

As I got older and became more interested in painting, I realized that there is no such thing as a single "flesh" color. Everybody's skin has many colors in it, and the way people look has a lot to do with how they're feeling at the time. I still love painting people, and I guess I'm still "coloring them in." My self-portrait is four different pictures of myself. I look different each time because I worked with four different kinds of artist's colors: oil paints, watercolors, colored pencils, and colored inks with oil pastels.

Daryl Wells was born in Los Angeles, California, in 1969, where she later worked with children creating outdoor murals. She has studied art in Rhode Island and London, England, and has taught art to children and adults of all ages.

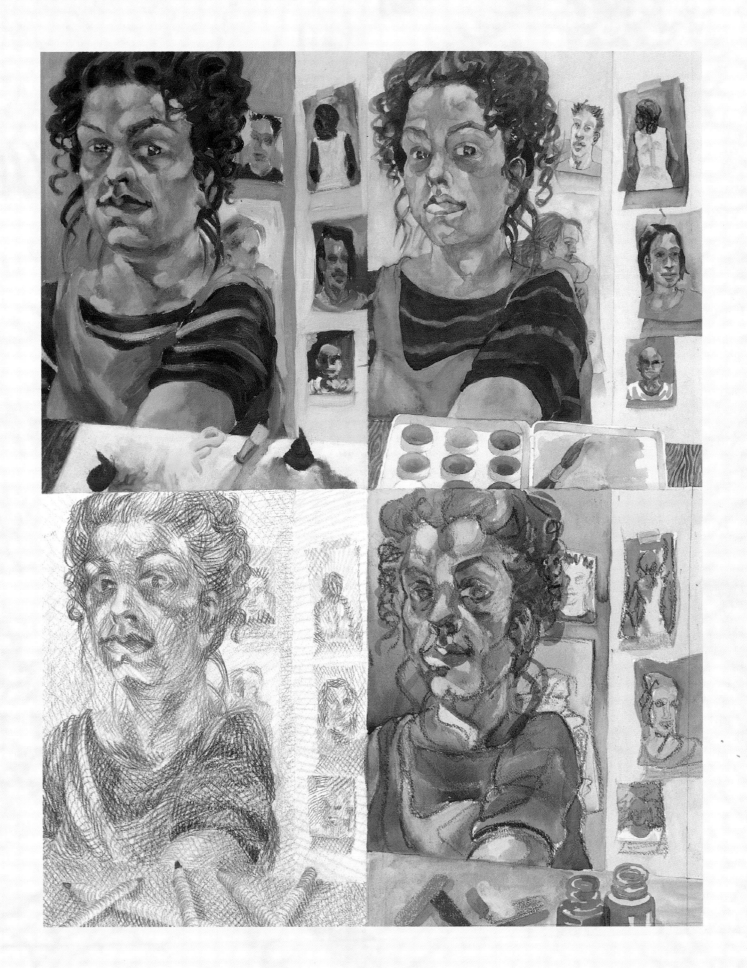

Michele Wood

As a child I often imagined myself as Sleeping Beauty, princess of the make-believe African kingdom of Koro. That's how I painted myself here. My hair is plaited in a royal crown of braids, and in my crown are six figures of me as paintbrushes showing different stages of my childhood. I'm playing with a hula hoop, riding a bike, reading storybooks, painting a picture, running track, and learning to sew.

The panels in the quilt show important times in my life. On the left, my mother is holding me as a baby. On the right, Mother and I are sitting on the kitchen floor playing jacks. I was an only child, and my mother would always participate in little games with me.

My character is a strong, fearless woman symbolizing the well-being of my people. I am free of fear, ready to forge ahead, hand in hand with my ancestors.

Michele Wood is a painter, printmaker, and mixed-media artist. She has recently been commissioned to create a mural celebrating Auburn Avenue, the heart of the historic African American community in Atlanta. Her work is shown in galleries in the United States and abroad. She was born in Indianapolis, Indiana, in 1964 and now lives in Atlanta, Georgia.

hideo Yoshida

When I pull back the curtain on my childhood, I see my uncle's pear orchard in the foothills of the Sierras. I'm ten or eleven years old—shirtless with a folded newspaper cap on my head to protect me from the sun. I remember the brilliant blue sky and the high, friendly puffs of clouds.

After I finished my morning task of hammering together 150 to 200 crates which we used to ship our pears to New York, I had the afternoon free. Then my cousin, my brother, and I would run off to go fishing in the streams and deep pools near the orchard.

When I do my work now, I long to feel what I felt then. I want to forget time and care only about what I'm trying to do at the moment. I want to be the way I am in this picture—a kid shirtless in the sun, putting one foot in front of the other, cautiously going forward.

Hideo Yoshida is a painter, printmaker, and mixed-media artist who was recently commissioned to document his family's history as farmers in California's Sacramento Valley. He was born in Sacramento, California, in 1942 and now lives in San Francisco, California.

About This Book

When I was just starting out in publishing, my dream was for all children to be able to open a book and see themselves. Back in 1975, that often didn't happen because very few books featured children of color, and fewer still were written or illustrated by authors and artists of color.

I was a single mother then, and my son was a Head Start student in the Mission District of San Francisco where people came from all over the world and spoke many different languages. We didn't have any books in our center that represented the cultures of the children, so I decided to work with artists from diverse communities to create our own books. That is the way I started working with the creative and committed group of artists you see in these pages.

The artists come from many different backgrounds and have traveled many different paths. Tomie Arai and Hideo Yoshida are the granddaughter and son of Japanese immigrant farmers. Nancy Hom was born in a village in China. Enrique Chagoya, Carmen Lomas Garza, Maya Christina Gonzalez, and Rodolfo Morales are Mexican and Mexican American artists of different generations and wildly different styles. George Littlechild was born in Canada of a Plains Cree mother and white father. Stephen Von Mason, JoeSam., Daryl Wells, and Michele Wood are African American artists who grew up in the Midwest, Harlem, and southern California at different times and create art in very different ways. Mira Reisberg and Elly Simmons grew up in working-class Jewish families in Australia and California.

As part of our publishing outreach program, we have always sent our artists into the schools—to teach children about art and literature and to act as role models. And it has been amazing to me how children are fascinated by artists. They see making art as some kind of magic and artists as magical people, and they want to know about them. "What do artists do?" they ask. "How did you become an artist? Where do you get your ideas? What were you like as a kid?"

Since I'm a publisher—always dreaming about the next beautiful book to create—I began to imagine a book that could bring these artists to a much wider audience. And so I decided to publish a book where the artists I have worked with would make pictures of themselves—and then talk about their self-portraits as a way of inspiring children to see art from a new perspective, as a way of showing children that artists come from many different places and work in many different ways.

The result is *Just Like Me: Stories and Self-Portraits by Fourteen Artists*. I hope this book will entertain and amuse you, give you food for thought, and inspire you with the ways in which these artists have remained true to their creative vision.

—**Harriet Rohmer**

Harriet Rohmer is the Publisher and Executive Director of Children's Book Press in San Francisco, California, the pioneering nonprofit publishing organization which she founded in 1975.

Just Like Me: Stories and Self-Portraits by Fourteen Artists

Tomie Arai (pp. 2–3)
Self-portrait medium: mixed media; adult photo by Legan Wong
Books for children:
China's Bravest Girl, Sachiko Means Happiness

Enrique Chagoya (pp. 4–5)
Self-portrait medium: watered-down acrylics
Books for children:
Mr. Sugar Came to Town/La visita del Sr. Azucar

Carmen Lomas Garza (pp. 6–7)
Self-portrait medium: acrylics; adult photo by Bob Hsiang
Books for children:
Family Pictures/Cuadros de familia, In My Family/En mi familia

Maya Christina Gonzalez (pp. 8–9)
Self-portrait medium: acrylics; adult photo by Lisi de Haas
Books for children:
Laughing Tomatoes and Other Spring Poems/Jitomates risuenos y otros poemas de primavera, Prietita and the Ghost Woman/Prietita y la Llorona

Nancy Hom (pp. 10–11)
Self-portrait medium: gouache; adult photo by Bob Hsiang
Books for children:
Judge Rabbit and the Tree Spirit, The Little Weaver of Thai-Yen Village, Nine-in-One, Grr! Grr!

George Littlechild (pp. 12–13)
Self-portrait medium: mixed media; adult photo by Matthew Jacobs, collage photos by Tom David Stratton, and child photo by Joanne Solamons
Books for children:
A Man Called Raven, This Land Is My Land

Stephen Von Mason (pp. 14–15)
Self-portrait medium: oils; adult photo by Tony Smith
Books for children:
Brother Anansi and the Cattle Ranch/El hermano Anansi y el rancho de ganado

Rodolfo Morales (pp. 16–17)
Self-portrait medium: collage; adult photo by Ariel Mendoza
Books for children:
Angel's Kite/La estrella de Angel

Mira Reisberg (pp. 18–19)
Self-portrait medium: acrylics; adult photo by Heidi Denton
Books for children:
Baby Rattlesnake, Elinda Who Danced in the Sky, Leaving for America, Uncle Nacho's Hat/El sombrero del tío Nacho, Where Fireflies Dance/Ahí, donde bailan las luciernagas

JoeSam. (pp. 20–21)
Self-portrait medium: mixed media; adult photo by Michael Jang
Books for children:
The Invisible Hunters/Los cazadores invisibles

Elly Simmons (pp. 22–23)
Self-portrait medium: mixed media
Books for children:
Calling the Doves/El canto de las palomas, Magic Dogs of the Volcanoes/Los perros magicos de los volcanes

Daryl Wells (pp. 24–25)
Self-portrait medium: mixed media; adult photo by Rob Trono
Books for children:
Two Mrs. Gibsons

Michele Wood (pp. 26–27)
Self-portrait medium: acrylics; adult photo by Bill Brooks
Books for children:
Going Back Home: An Artist Returns to the South

Hideo Yoshida (pp. 28–29)
Self-portrait medium: acrylics; adult photo by Hideo Yoshida
Books for children:
Why Rat Comes First

All children's books listed above are available through Children's Book Press.

Consulting Editor: David Schecter   Design/Production: John Miller and Eleanor Reagh, Big Fish   Editorial/Production Assistant: Laura Atkins

Thanks to the staff of Children's Book Press: Janet Levin, Emily Romero, Stephanie Sloan, and Christina Tarango

Children's Book Press is a nonprofit publisher of multicultural literature for children, supported in part by grants from the California Arts Council.
Write us for a complimentary catalog:
Children's Book Press, 246 First Street, Suite 101, San Francisco, CA 94105, (415) 995-2200.

Distributed to the book trade by Publishers Group West

Library of Congress Cataloging-in-Publication Data
Just like me: stories and self-portraits by fourteen artists; edited by Harriet Rohmer   p. cm.   Summary: Fourteen artists and picture book illustrators present self-portraits and brief descriptions that explore their varied ethnic origins, their work, and how they feel about themselves.   ISBN 0-89239-149-9 (hardcover) 1. Self-portraits—Juvenile literature. 2. Artists—Psychology—Juvenile literature. [1. Artists. 2. Self-portraits.]   I. Rohmer, Harriet.   N7618.J87 1997   704.9'42—DC21   97-4467   CIP   AC

Printed in Singapore by Tien Wah Press
10 9 8 7 6 5 4 3 2 1